Passage

(Átutazás)

Passage
(Átutazás)

Poems

Tony Reevy

Iris Press
Oak Ridge, Tennessee

Cover Photo Credit: *Woman (probably Hungarian) coming home along railroad tracks in coal mining town, company houses at right, Pursglove, Scotts Run, West Virginia.* Photo by Marion Post Wolcott, September 1938. Library of Congress, Prints and Photographs Division, FSA-OWI Collection, LC-USF33-030285-M1.

Book Design by Robert B. Cumming, Jr.

Library of Congress Cataloging-in-Publication Data

Reevy, Tony.
  [Poems. Selections]
  Passage (atutazas) / Tony Reevy.
      pages ; cm
  ISBN 978-1-60454-229-5 (softcover : acid-free paper)
  I. Title.
  PS3618.E4459A6 2015
  811'.6—dc23
                                    2015003026

Acknowledgements

The author would also like to acknowledge the following publications where several of these poems first appeared, or are pending publication:

Bath Avenue Newsletter: "The Survivor"
Blood and Honey Review: "First Papers"
Crab Orchard Review: "View from the Eastland Hotel"
The Iconoclast: "Death of Attila József"
Lightning in Wartime (Georgetown, Kentucky: Finishing Line Press, 2007): "Conquest"
Magdalena (Columbus, Ohio: Pudding House Publications, 2004): "Black Land," "The Boy's First Flight"
National Slovak Society Almanac: "Sklabina Castle"
Off the Coast: "Lament of the Muse," "Puszta," "Uncle Bus"
Out of Line: "Ellis Island Ferry"
Pembroke Magazine: "Stars of Eger," "View from the St. John Church"
Say It at Your Wedding: "Dancing the Csárdás"
Spillway: "Prize of War"
Windhover: "Hungarian Views," "The Glider Pilot"

As in the past, many thanks to my poetry group—Bruce, Geni, Korki and Renata, to my family, and to my editors—Bob at Iris Press, Laura at ABRAMS and Linda and Sarah at Indiana University Press.

To my parents,
Carole and Bill Reevy

Contents

IV   Looking Backward

I

Prelude (1848/1849)

You cannot forbid the flower

Sándor Petőfi (1823-1849): Poet of the Hungarian National Uprising against the Hapsburgs, killed in battle.

Red blossom
planted by cavalry saber
or cannon ball or bullet

So it was done—

Like Mozart, to a mass
grave, while the Russian doctor
took notes.

Some say the poet
was force-marched to Siberia,
or, brain-bullet-stricken,

wandered Debrecen streets,
penniless, muttering verses,
his hand out for alms.

II

Emigrants/Immigrants

Prize of War

1866

The Prussians had fast rifles,
we had muzzle-loaders.
Now, the war was over,

and those who lived
struggled across Silesia,
over the Tatras, to our land.

I brought my new woman,
a Pole, her belly as swollen
as a knapsack—young,

slim, long hair, full-baubled
chest, sometimes laughing
in the pines.

My army pack, coin pouch,
sinking lower as we walked
the long miles home.

Passage (Átutazás)

When Father died, János got the holding.
Mama spoke me for the Church—
but that was not to be.

Even at sixteen, I loved the company
of women, their dark glances,
the csárda, too much to turn priest.

János lent me the ticket money.
Of the stinking boat, the hell
of Castle Garden, I try not to think.

A long road to a house, a mine—my
own—and the mists of these green
Amerikai Pennsylvania hills.

UMW Strike

The Cossacks, Yellow Dogs, rode us
down, flailing with clubs. I saw
one reach for his holster.

Couldn't spare their horses
any more. Dumped my tin
bucket—the ball bearings

toppled their mounts. We
stepped up with pick handles,
baseball bats. Put our muscles,

swollen from loading tons
a day, to work against
blue-hatted heads.

Dancing the Csárdás

I swore I'd never step
on a big ship again.

The swaying, dim light
below decks, people seasick.

And on and on we sailed.

Father said *He's a big man,
a Magyar, doing well in America—*
and I thought I could remember
the boy running by our house.

Mother closed my hope chest,
said goodbye at the station.

Father went with me,
and brother János, to Fiume
on the smoke-spitting train.

And, at the Island,
when I got through,
he was there, standing
at the bottom of the stairs.

Then the train, the church,
it was done.

A life—a good life?
I guess it was.

He was a good man—
we had children,
some moved on, some
stood by us
at the end.

The work was hard, long,
but we danced the csárdás
when we could.

Dispatch from the Front

War correspondent with the Serbian army, 1914

The Austrian trenches
were hemmed with wire
at the front and rear

to keep the Czechs from running

as they shot Servians—
their Slav brothers—
before them.

Passing

Endre Ady, Hungarian poet, 1877-1919, born in Érmindszent, died in Budapest. The lines from "The Hackney Coach" are as translated by Anton N. Nyerges (in Adam Makkai, editor, In Quest of the Miracle Stag *(Budapest: Corvina, 1996), p. 401).*

As Entente tanks rumble
up from Salonika
and the Bulgarians throw down
their guns

while Romanians saunter the streets
of Pest, breaking windows
and turning up dresses
in tenement alleys

The Hackney Coach rider
shuts himself in a room,
liver, kidneys racked by wine,
brain a syphilitic mass

with new wife, who loved his poems,
now the man—

*Never before has a mortal pair
so striven for the peaks of life,
and none was ever more threadbare.*

—and nothing can be consummated anymore.

She sponges his brow
as breath stills.

To the West

He sold the mine, number Thirteen,
to buy an old-country home
after guns stilled,

and hauled his boys, girls,
Americans now, *speaking the English*,
back to nervous stares
from new gendarmes,

and from councilors, who turned
hand and cane
to put boot on throat
of the former leaders

with their impaling stakes,
meat hooks, impossible language
forced down native throats.

The time was not right
to return like a lord
to a homeland forever changed,
while he had looked
to mines and money
in the West.

Shepherd's Fold, High Tatras

The High Tatras are a mountain range on the border between Slovakia and Poland; until 1920, they were part of Upper Hungary (a term now offensive to most Slovaks) in Austria-Hungary. The Tatra Mountains were used in the 18th and 19th centuries for sheep grazing and mining and many trees were cut down to make way for human exploitation.

To Charlie (Károly)

Hunt or go hungry—
easier in misted morn.

Dewed-grass tracks—
still mountain meadow.

Flinging stick tight-gripped,
cloak pulled close.

Track rabbit tree-ward,
silent as soft breeze.

Brushed branch at forest edge—
hare streaks away.

Watch sun glint and blink
through falling mist.

First Papers

Declarations of Intention (or First Papers): Normally the first papers were completed soon after arrival in the U.S., depending on the laws in effect at the time.

When I looked from the window,
hearing the sound of horses,
I saw the gendarmes
sent by my own brother
at the gate.

Knew the last owner of my house,
a royalist—and the flat
wooden cases of rifles
buried in the yard.

The land was ours no longer—
I blessed the day
I'd signed papers saying
I could stay in a new land
if I lived.

Clash of gun butt
against wood told me
it was time
to open the door.

Ellis Island Ferry

I'm remembering it—bedlam. The
stinking launches, blue-coat
officers like Emperor's men.
Lines, screaming ones
turned away. At the end, railroad
men, more blue-coats, one-way
tickets to the Youngstown mill.

My father's neck, pitted with
deep round burns, told the rest
of the story.

Today, we stand in the ferry's bow,
the waters purr by. I squeeze my
granddaughter's hand, my fingers
a creaking claw. She looks up,
sharp—I'm hurting her. How to
tell about the stench, the massed
people. I was a snip of a thing,
too young to hope.

The gorge of my fear rises
as we step off the boat; the
fear takes my eyes and I turn
from the little one to hide my
old face, now young, a boy
again, dirty, hungry, here.

The Mule Driver Leaves the Mine

It was Klára I cared for
in that dark hole.

When the rock fall
took her, it got my

leg—but I could
have worked on.

The mines are not
my place anymore.

Burning

Anti-Catholicism was widespread in the 1920s; anti-Catholics, including the Ku Klux Klan, believed that Catholicism was incompatible with democracy and that parochial schools encouraged separatism and kept Catholics from becoming loyal Americans.

Sudden night-fire-cross,
like unwanted sun,
flames on hill crest
crowning home vale
and farm fields.

Horses snort
in their stalls.
Dog barks at the
unseen invader.
Mother stares out

the window, murmurs
in Slovak,
pod' sem, shelters
the boy
under her full skirt.

The Debt (A Tartozás)

Creosote smell, ties spaced
just wrong for my
footfalls. Mama walking
the rails with me, thirteen
miles to Portage. No
train today, mines running
just twice a week.

Uncle's house, doilies
under the lamps. But Mama
and me come back
with no money. Pap,
yelling, *Never go there
again. I paid his way
to Amerika. He's no
brother of mine now.*

I run out to the spring,
watch the crystal water
spill and gurgle, hold
my hand in till
it's numb.

The Maid's Room

Top of the stairs, closeted,
iron bedstead, washstand
with pitcher and bowl,

Catholic bible—*Mary can
read*—wood-bead black
rosary alongside, to finger

at bedtime or in a long
night. Framed litho
of Jesus on bare white

wall. Like her sisters,
she's just here at night,
a place for sleeping

after a day of scrubbing,
sweeping. Sunday's quiet,
one day off each month.

Sunday Csárdás

Wood crackles in the stove,
and smoke mixed
with cabbage boil reeks.

Kitchen winter-cold despite
the fire. Ma is rolling
halupki. Pap walks up

behind her, clasps
her waist. She looks
up, turns to him

and they dance csárdás
without music, brogans
and high-buttons

thumping, slapping on kitchen
plank floor. The fiddle's
in the corner,

and there it stays—even
Pap can't dance
and play at once.

III

In a New World

The Boy's First Flight

The beacon went up
in the south forty—
lighting the way for
Jennies carrying mail.

One of the pilots
on the route
made extra money
working stunts at fairs.

He took the boy up,
free—in the second
cockpit, where they
stuffed the loads.

High over fields,
mountains, boney
piles. Everything
new and clean.

That birdman blazed
from the sky one
night. Shouldn't have
gone out—but, after the

Huns, he thought he
had a charm. The boy
had to be told. Fence
riders don't always

come back. Someday,
the Ranger or Tonto,
one of them, will
have to ride on alone.

Death of Attila József

Hungarian poet, born Budapest, 1905, died Balatonszárszó, 1937

The poet takes a walk,
leaves the brother's house—
a Royal Army guard stares.

The path narrows downward,
to the tracks and Balaton.

A train starts
                    from the station.

Engine driver doesn't feel
the slight tug—
a body caught
                    in vise grip
then cut, parted.

Heart pumps free—
then, drained, stops.

Blood clots
            on cold rails.

The hard journey
from Ferencváros, Szeged
ends here,
                sudden and tragic,
alone.

Childbed Fever

Medicine bottles forgotten
on the washstand, mattress
piled with bloodied bedsheets
burning in the woods.

The second sister
stoops to scrub wooden
floorboards. The funeral
is over; newborn wails

in the nursery the lost
mother prepared months
ago. The father stands
at the window, sees boney

piles, men passing—home
from the mine. Sisters-
in-law will look after the baby,
but for how long? All

will expect him to remarry,
God's will, but after such love
he cannot imagine
it so.

MP Shot by Italian POW

The Italians worked defense production
at the mill—and that day
one didn't get back to camp.

The detail buckled on their gun
belts. Horvath looked forward
to the hunt, to serving the flag.

The Wop was on the sidewalk
by the Carolina, waiting
for a movie.

Horvath ran up, shouted—Wop
stiff-armed him, grabbed his gun.
They grappled; bullet ploughed

through Horvath's foot. Rest
of the detail beat the Wop down
while Horvath screamed.

*The way he treated his kid, wife,
he deserved to be shot—
God's will.*

Years later, wearing his adjunct
deputy badge, a purple heart, at lodge
picnics, Horvath told it different—

and it got him VA benefits
for life.

The Lost Cousins

*The Russians rapidly destroyed the Hungarian Second Army near Svoboda on
the Don River [in January and February 1943]*

Crusted slush along the freeway
brings to mind not Bing
and a white Christmas
but mile-less frozen wastes
beyond the Don

where infantry armed with rifles,
if they had been armed at all,
freezing in a bitter land,
were transformed to red
spots in the snow—fiber, faces

pulped under Red Army tanks,
just pawns in the game.

Lament of the Muse

On the death of Miklós Radnóti, Hungarian poet (born Budapest, 1909; died near Abda, 1944)

He staggers, collapses.
The labor-camp crews

                        stare.

Not fit for *Arbeit*

                    anymore.
A bullet.

Euterpe lifts her wings

                    wearily,
only to let them fall.

I don't go

to those reunions cause
eighty out of a hundred
guys in my unit
didn't come back.

I was in the infantry.

One time, after they shipped
me home, I went
to a buddy's funeral—

stepped through the viewing
line, his mother
standing there. She says

*That should be you
in the coffin.*

So, I don't go back.

A Lost Cousin, Found

The radio said they were liberators.
Not so. I don't tell, but I remember,
as a girl of thirteen, my skirt pulled
down to my ankles, bunched
there, then torn and tossed.

And the Red Army men taking
their turns at me. So it was
with my sisters, of blood
and tongue, and so it was
I crossed, under Devín's guns,

the revolution dying around me,
to the other side
of the curtain.

Last at the Scene

Green-clad Catskills clasp the road—
bank to the left and fall
to a stream on the right.

Early mist rises, the whine
of a milk tanker, a car
revs to pass—

two sedans meet. No jaws
of life—troopers free the bodies
with crowbars.

After the meatwagons, a cop
measures skid marks; the tow-truck driver
sweeps glass into a pan—

dumps the mess down the embankment,
takes off gloves, wipes hands.
Another late breakfast today.

Inmate at the State Hospital

Raindrops sluice down the pane—
there's always a scream—
but she sits still on the bed

gazing through bars. They removed
restraints years ago. But she
won't die yet. Thunderbolt claps,

rattles window, she starts—
draws sharp breath.
Lunch tray untouched

beside her—Salisbury steak,
peas, milk, jello.
She'll have to eat soon

or they'll force-feed. For one minute,
though, sun breaks through
thin, scudding clouds.

The Lost Children

The State took their mother,
heart-wounded by their father,
to the asylum.

And took them to history—
three gone, adopted away
from their name.

Not to be found, unless they,
or their offspring, if any,
look to the past.

After seventy-five years,
there's no word—no stories
of the war, or of children

born in the forties, fifties,
even sixties, marriages,
passings—

no contact, not even
when their mother died
in a state hospital bed.

Housecleaning

Flames rise from steamer trunk
in the backyard—oldest
daughter piles on papers, mildewed
needlework, her father's pipe.

Farmhouse needs a good scrub
now that Ma's gone;
and Pap, alone at the end,
in an old-folks' home.

Toss on the refuse—passports,
photos, deeds to houses farms mines
long since sold.

Postcards—the ship that brought
them over, harbor at Fiume—
flip into the fire.

They curl, vent foul-smelling
spume, light—
fly off in a wisp
of bitter ash.

Funeral Day

For a grandfather I never met

The kitchen seemed warm
after playing in the lake-effect
snow. Dad loomed over
the table, clad in unfamiliar
dark suit. Picked up his keys,

kissed Mom. Then we
watched him drive off
in the red Plymouth Valiant
that didn't have as many fins
as the other boys' daddies'

cars. And Mom and I stood
at the window looking
for a long time, till Mom
turned away, said *I still wonder
if we should have gone.*

Uncle Bus

Brick-patterned
tar-paper town
ringed by boney piles
smoking from their weight.
Uncle Bus lived there.

Remembered in a photo:
Bus home from the mine,
raccoon-eyed, slumped.
Taken in bad times—wife, three
kids, two days work a week.

Thirty years on, I loved to visit,
to haunt the cast cement-block
store and post office,
to trace the intricate, rusty
ironwork of the tipple.

One time, I dragged things
home to Bus's: lard
bucket, coat hanger. Junk.
Strung them on a guy-wire:
tipple buckets lifting coal.

No dice. Bus—only time
I saw him angry—
made me haul it all away.
*Idle hands are the
devil's workshop.*

Bus didn't understand.
Or maybe, just maybe,
he didn't see a reason
to play at building
the mine.

Now—coughed and gone—
my uncle, the mine, the
whole bloody mess. Only
the stilled town and its
boney piles, smoking, remain.

The Survivor

The spring ran
beside the upper forty.
Its small, cold pool
dammed by a pine board.

Mossed and wet-black,
set by my grandfather
forty years before.

I touched the plank,
tough but supple,
there beyond its years.

Imagined a man with
a tin dipper of water;
a boy, my father,
leading the horse here to drink.

Thirty years ago, now,
I saw the survivor;
tasted the cool, sharp water
my father drank every day.

I guess the board's gone now;
the spring likely dry.
I plan to find the spot;
and long to let memory be.

Greenpoint, Brooklyn, 1974

The family got together
at the Greenpoint Avenue
block party.

Everyone brought a case
of Schlitz
except Uncle John, who brought whiskey
and wine.

His address was Columbus
                              Circle.

The boy walked around a long
corner with him—they avoided
the Avenue.

They discussed the future,
engineering and Cooper
                              Union.

Back at the brownstone, Aunt Mary
(married to Uncle Charlie)
showed the boy her son's
layouts (thuggish good looks)

in *Modern Romance*,
pulp-paper already brittle—

Uncle John
had *already seen*
those articles.

So had the boy's Dad
and Mom, professor
and teacher.

It was the last time
the brothers gathered.

Aunt Julia

The old men shovel mud
from basements, flooded again,
as my family flashes through Johnstown
in a 1973 tin-box Maverick,
headed for the hills.

To Nanty Glo village, where Julia,
related to me somehow—
I don't get it at fifteen—
plies me with noodles and butter
and paprika.

My little sisters, mother
ignored on the couch
as Julia chitters, incomprehensible
language—to my dad,
who makes halting replies.

And to me, in English thick
with unknown accent,
Julia says, *Eat, eat.* Feeling
my thin arm, poking my side:
Eat, eat.

Bus Brown's Funeral

Seventies tin-box car
crawl-climbs peaks, snakes
the Shenandoah vale, past
Winchester Blue and Gray
Motel, west of Broad Top
to tiny coal town.

At ex-company house,
whiff of boney-pile smoke
as women and men gather
to lay Bus
in the ground.

This black-lunged man
who labored in the Earth
each workday—
or two days a week
in Hoover times.

It's a long road from *Auld
Reekie* brought this man, chest
wizened like a dried apple,
to a churchyard undercut
by company tunnels.

Where no one can stop
the craters swallowing lawns,
playgrounds as dark rocks
shift far below.

Thirteen

Some say it was a trolley stop
thirteen halts out of Barnesboro—
others tell of a shaft
between mines Twelve and Fourteen.

Charlie scouted out the foundations—
the long, narrow one a boarding house,
the squat squares miners' homes—
and flat slip of vanished railroad
speckled with ballast stones.

It was his last hunting trip
to the old homeplace
before black lung and cigarettes
cut him down.

He couldn't find the mine,
its black mouth gaping
for men to enter.

When November mist rises
in those Pennsylvania hills
it can still seem that
something's there.

The Glider Pilot

From round, green hills,
at eighteen,
strapped into
an aluminum shell,
powerless, propless.

Dropped in deep jungle
of rustlings
that chilled more
than comic-book Japs
back in the States.

Took a year in the VA
to get ready for home,
for the mines, the
slate creaks and groans.

Work, strange truth,
he liked—and not
just because it put
food on the table.

His daughters,
one on each side, lead
him to a pew.
Alone, stunned like a
deer in the spots.

After jungle runs,
roof falls,
his helmet crushed
flat as a dinner plate.

After buddies wheezing
last breaths through
dust-laced lungs.

Who'd have thought
she'd go first.

Black Land

On the edge
of town orange water
seeps from a dark
drift hole

rimmed by false
hills of boney tied
with rusted rails
to nothing.

Trees fringe clearcut
and slate lumps.
At least the mountain,
a honeycomb, still rises,

towers above houses
laid together, identical
shells cloaking
history under

vinyl, aluminum, stucco,
spots of festive paint,
added rooms, trellised
porches, shrines, lawns:

as demobilized regiments,
removing uniforms,
become patchwork,
human, again.

IV

Looking Backward

I didn't know

my granddaddy. Didn't
know rock dust
grating between
his fingers, smell of
stuffed cabbage at
late dinner, coal
smoke seeping
from kitchen

range. I didn't know
my granddaddy, didn't
know vomit stench of
steerage, seasick
swing of cots, steady
dim light below
decks. I didn't
know my grand-
daddy, didn't know

Castle Spirit

Rise from the meathook, ghost.
Don't ask what the past means to you.
The time for temptation is lost,
Days gone are left for the few.

The forest beckons with leaves,
That shift as the wind sifts the trees.
Go there to seek new times,
Do not linger to punish the new.

These children's grandparents weren't born,
When bullets ploughed these fields.
The sword was drawn against babies,
Bring not this curse on anew.

Gypsy

Shuffling gait
from glasses
of Bikavér, Leanka;
playing violin
for tourists'
shillings and marks.

Behind—no money,
war's wire camps,
sickle-hammer chorus.
Today—wine, warm, three
hundred forints, bread.
Tomorrow—another sun.

View from the St. John Church

Ebon branches of
dying locust:
dark lattice
flecked with green.

Long struggle
with borers and rot:
often noted
by painters and tourists.

Below, red-tiled
roofs, stuccoed walls,
cobbled passageways:
Szentendre town.

Beyond, brown
Duna, drifting slow,
heedless of time,
to the sea.

Hungarian Views

1. Turkish minaret, Eger

Boney finger;
single survivor
presented to a
willing heaven.

2. World War II veteran, Sopron

Wine bar;
reddened glass
held by
three-fingered man.

3. Modern art museum, Pécs

Sculpture garden,
weed grown, crowded:
forgotten idols,
broken age.

János Révay, In Retirement

Five years after the fall of the Wall

The former commissar
of Slovenský Raj tourism
plies us with slivovitz.

Already tipsy at mid-
afternoon, he splashes
it into what we'd call
shot glasses.

That's what everyone does
for an Amerikai-Magyar
and his szép wife.

The question of the hour,
how a Hungarian came
to this position in Slovakia,
lies on the table unvoiced.

How are things?

I am a pensioner now,
János says, in German,
and lifts his glass.

Blatnica

We could not reach the
castle, but must imagine
the glade where ruins lie
mossy-black against the
sky. Clouds scud the
Tatras, lower at dusk to
mist the dark rocks, the
gapped tower. Ebon spots
emerge against dying
sun, while ravens
return to their roosts.

Soon, owls will hunt
clearings footing
the castle-crowned
outcrop. The kin that trod
this keep are gone and,
even knowing where it
lies, we cannot walk the
path to its hold.

Next morning, the sun
rises; bats give place
to jet-winged watchers
for another day.

Sklabina Castle

A smoke-feather
winds upwards
from the gatehouse.

Doorway to
walls opened
by the bomb.

Survivor of the blast,
the fire,
the timbers and stones
spinning to the sky.

The caretaker explains:
Meaningless sounds;
and the language of ancestors.

Understanding vanishes
in a new world.

Stars of Eger

I lift the window,
a hatch in the roof;
find stars, more stars
than waves on the sea.
Dotted over church,
castle: still
peace in the night.

The sill is hard, with
sharp edges; the air
chill and dry.
A clock chimes the half
of some single-digit hour.

Thousands died here.
The castle moat clogged
with muck wetted by blood.

I grip the sill harder,
the edge cutting my palm.
Learning the death of thousands
leaves no mark.

In the everyday turns
of this world
screams fade to flowers
pushing through the rocks.

Conquest

The castle rampart
rims a hill over-
looking Vérmező.

Déli station's
signals glimmer
red, green below.

Turks, Austrians,
Germans, Russians
scaled this low wall.

Each war-tide
receded with
time. In the

valley, trams
clang at Moszkva
tér, people bustle

to the Metro.
The lights of a
McDonalds glow.

Slovakia at the End of the Curtain

Fresh vegetables so scarce
they are kept
in the grocery's
display case.

The Musician Visits Transylvania (Erdély)

I can tell who is Magyar,
Gypsy, on the bus—
the Romanians move over, away,
seeing my darker skin, eyes,
hearing my tortured
mother tongue.

View from the Eastland Hotel

Portland, Maine

Stars like pinholes
fill the window—a lighthouse
calls to the sea.

Shades of tall-masted clippers
could crowd this dark harbor—
or steel ships such as brought
the one remembered tomorrow
to this far place.

Inside, where it's warm, waiters—
imported from the former
Soviet Union—hover. A man
and woman drink together,
lean close, his hand on her skirt.

Alone, I sit and watch
another Russian, with
three men, uncrossing and
re-crossing smooth, shaped legs.

The beacon flares again, as
I plan the next day
of this windward visit,
tempting shoals in this
port of the dead.

Portland, Me. Funeral

In memory of John Reevy

These tall strangers were blurs
on a boat—a ship,
really, the *Queen Mary*—
when last I saw them,
their father and mother.

This is their father's
funeral—my home's
a thousand miles south.
I have no connection
to this place—but this place
is everything to them.

The minister gives a homily
for the dead man, talks
of his descent into a burning
engine room, his taking in
a nephew as less-able hands
reached for the boy. Some
are old stories, oft-told
by my father, others
new as day.

Afterwards, I gun
the rented car south, hop
a plane. There are plans
to meet, but I know I may
never see these people,
this place again.

On Great-Aunt's Wall

The little girl is frightened
by the crucifix,
Jesus nailed and pierced.

Red-paint blood flows
like river of ages
and faith of the days.

Puszta (Waste)

Scrap paper drifts across the parking lot
where furnace blasts once lit the sky.

Empty windows in the strip mall
gape at the road.

The hotel's an old folks home—a man
mumbles on the stoop.

The train station's a thrift store, tracks pared
from many to one.

And the Paprika Restaurant's now
a greasy spoon—

Fires laid down, seven hundred
tons of steel a day
crumble to rust.

New Lake at Dedinky, Slovakia

Old church still stands
on the hill, but houses
just below are new.

A city thirsted.
The village has moved
to higher ground.

Road runs arrow-
straight to the reservoir
and ends at its shore.

Grey water ripples
the bank. Below, carp
feed beside algae-

encrusted lane passing
chimney stones that once
warmed old men.

A Pasture in Slovakia

Dull rustle of
wind through
last, late-winter

leaves reminds me
of dim shades
dancing on Révay's

field—grazed,
green rectangle
beyond the sea.

No context—
the dancers are
ghosts, their bright

costumes—white, black,
crimson, violet, emerald—
fading grey. The

key is lost, the root
is here now
or nowhere.

The seeds are
scattered, the stream
runs under rocks and

clay. The root is
here now, or
nowhere.

Ruins in Two Continents

Sklabina Castle, in Slovakia, was destroyed by the Nazis during World War II.
The old Durham, North Carolina pump station was abandoned after a new
water system was built in the 1920s.

A rook calls
from shattered keep;
dark forest fills
lone castle-cleft
in cragged mountains.

Westwards, full river rushes
by ruined walls; a boy walks
homeward, hand-in-hand
with Father, searching
the ground for tracks.

Senior associate director of the Institute for the Environment at the University of North Carolina at Chapel Hill, Tony Reevy (Révay in Hungarian) is a graduate of North Carolina State University, UNC-Chapel Hill and Miami University. He is a David P. Morgan Award winner (2006) and a Pushcart Prize nominee. His previous publications include poetry, non-fiction and short fiction, including the non-fiction books *Ghost Train!* and *O. Winston Link: Life Along the Line*; the full book of poetry, *Old North*; and the poetry chapbooks *Green Cove Stop, Magdalena, Lightning in Wartime*, and *In Mountain Lion Country*. His latest non-fiction book, *The Railroad Photography of Jack Delano*, is pending from Indiana University Press. Reevy's father is Hungarian, Slovak and Polish, and was born in Dobsina, Slovakia (then Czechoslovakia). Reevy resides in Durham, North Carolina with wife, Caroline Weaver, and children Lindley and Ian.